Sky Lounge

Sky Lounge

Mark Bibbins

Graywolf Press
SAINT PAUL, MINNESOTA

Publication of this volume is made possible in part by a grant provided by the Minnesota State Arts Board, through an appropriation by the Minnesota State Legislature; a grant from the Wells Fargo Foundation Minnesota; and a grant from the National Endowment for the Arts. Significant support has also been provided by the Bush Foundation; Marshall Field's Project Imagine with support from the Target Foundation; the McKnight Foundation; and other generous contributions from foundations, corporations, and individuals. To these organizations and individuals we offer our heartfelt thanks.

Special funding for this title has been provided by the Jerome Foundation.

Published by Graywolf Press
2402 University Avenue, Suite 203
Saint Paul, Minnesota 55114

www.graywolfpress.org

Published in the United States of America

ISBN 1-55597-380-9

2 4 6 8 9 7 5 3 1
First Graywolf Printing, 2003

Library of Congress Control Number: 2002111749

Cover design: Kyle Hunter

Cover art: Marco Breuer, *Tremors (#5)*, 2000.
        Courtesy of Roth Horowitz Gallery

Contents

1

So much flesh in the world
Wanders at will

—Mina Loy

Just Yesterday

Before prayer in the schools we had the Crusades
and we cleaned out the stockpot once a year.

Virtually everything we ate induced narcosis,
a condition we often confused with god.

Some told of a river that ran outside the city walls
and of how it moved to avoid their touch,

a giant serpent twisting forever away. If it wasn't the devil
it was the work of the devil like everything else we wanted.

Remorse held us together until we died young
and most of us never realized we were mammals—

indeed we were suspicious of birds but rats, well, rats
we found charming, with their eyes so full

of sympathy, their need for warmth like our own. We also
wanted love to suffice. Flies that collected on the lesions

of the dying: angels one and all: no one could be too careful.
It seemed a flood was forever rinsing ideas from my tongue

so I said nothing or spoke louder, I was always drowning.
I couldn't have changed anything.

All right there was the alchemist
and I loved him but I could not save him.

Once I dreamt of electricity. Was this the river,
the one that altered its course like a wounded thing?

We had no trees, only sticks.
Huge gears turned in the sky.

If Not to Speak Against

All paintings are of trees or should
be. From the Urdu word for dust

comes the color of the uniform.
All songs are about love.

We position so others cannot see
then lie and call it contact.

We measure the length of the shore
and say don't look at the water.

An army moves across a desert
in olive drab, through clouds of dust.

What's topical becomes generic,
for instance bombs

that look like food fall from the sky
and land near people living on dust.

Anyone in the painting, hiding behind
a tree, is presumed to be a lover.

Attire is protection, idiom, antagonism.
All photographs depict the black fins

of whales as they go under.
No one can be counted on

to water the office trees.
Submitting to systems is autonomy

as long as systems vary, as long
as what's generic is topical.

All but Lost

My love lives down by the butchery,
at night he keeps coins on his eyes.

When we were still called children
I clothed myself in hides and relished

the generators that shook the ground.
Tesla didn't like jewelry, couldn't bear

to touch human hair and claimed
to have destroyed his sexuality

at the age of 40 but of course everyone
was doing that then.

I sang Piaf songs
till they burned my tongue — precocious is

as precocious does — the French
all but lost to me now. Fate

presented itself as a ghost I could smell
under the floorboards as I listened

to mice gnawing on books I had
already memorized. When the doctor put

leeches on my torso he made no effort
to hide his arousal or the anisette

on his breath. He said I would
not die yet. He said the martyr's

a murderer locked in a room
till the saint slips him the key.

Euphorium

1. Slipping Mickeys

The fact of men liplocked makes him
want to flee.
Springboard, perspiration,

the accumulated winter
blasted away. An invert song
pulled into wire, an old map poorly

drawn but not unlovely—we'll
make it there by dark. I was born
with capable eyes,

a movable heart
and time to spare. Surely
he must know something

of the icy language we're in?
At night we paced by the door,
waiting for guests

who never came. We made
ever-wider circles around the house,
our wails scalding the trees,

the moon, the blue of our veins,
the blue pull as boys and other boys
dissolved at levels we couldn't see.

2. Intrusion

I once relied too heavily upon
the green undulations

of the worm on the garden
hose, the sag of rhododendron.

The elders have recently
decided (humor them)

to let go of the lingo a little.
Oh it's easy to blame

the one with the widest mouth,
the one who appears to have

gotten there first. We are not
disposed to be bored, despite.

I'm looking for something
that's one-third comma, two-thirds question

mark. I wonder if they're hiding
anything like that around here,

maybe among the unmentionables
drying on the rod?

3. El Super-Guapo

(a.k.a. Outhouse Crank Diva)
shows the world beauty
is neither fleeting nor quantifiable.
Switch stylists, light will cradle the body.
I've only to look at something and it tangles—
the boyfriend overheating, for instance, smug,
not "seeing" the "hustler"—we've come that far—
but he turns down the radio so he can learn
the notorious effects of steroids
upon temperament and testicles:
that could be the banner or banter under which no one's
first summer lurches and strains.
Envy the sand he covers now and trade in smart for wise,
a shell to my ear, the same goofy hat.
Who wouldn't have preferred a longer June?
Only flirt for one reason and make your exit.
Make it into sand and shape. Feed it a cold sea.
Pimps and fisherfolk and bold moves,
such salty skin he disappears.

Doldrums

So much in need of repair piles up —
        this week the country is cross
with certain perverts and why not.

Four A.M. titillates, the rails
loosen and contract with secret import.

Righteous indignation, my favorite kind.
The shouts of tourists
wedge the air. Consolation lies
in the dunes, a nuzzle or two.

Fueled by je ne sais quoi,
I'm distracted by cruising

cars with rockabilly flair — not to mention
the crappy verse adorning my leg cast —
as I hobble into the intersection.

It's easy to read
the lines here — amoeboid,
another drags by,
        unprecedented skin.

The sky turns narcotic, vast,
and the Wonder Wheel rolls into the sea.

Arrival with Dark Circles and Premonition

Trompe l'oeil   under the bridge   trumps the meth-head

on the bus   who's dragged himself   from southern climes

to find the earth's curve   barely registers here.

Say he wanted something   and it was refinement

or a city   on a map   through which he could burn

a hole   or a garland of houses   woven through a field.

Doctors once held him   upside down

to get   the poison out   a man

with blue toenails   assured him a city   is just an idea.

Say his name   is Jared or Zak

bumper-sticker vandal   T-shirt philosopher

tracking a god that's nothing

more than sleep   with schnapps and dregs

of opium   scraped from foil.   When he wakes up

in a park at dawn   where armored cars   sail the sky

say all the statues   have moved

have turned   to look at him.

Tingling in the Extremities

Here is a misplaced forecast from the spring:

a big Sorry in the alfresco restaurant,
his whole posse gathered to see
what he's become.

Nothing worth repeating
        over the tin-can telephone,
the one he loves fills his water glass
and is gone.

He cuts his finger on the lobster shell
and glides down the walk. Swift now.

A summer of traffic,
                the stereo works
and the sun cooperates.

                        He is forever going down
                for the sand, the air quivers
and holds bodies aloft.

The music blurs and everyone
is in on it.

        You'll love our m-m-malts.
        "I love a promise," he confides.

He has forgotten the need
for transitions,

or hasn't learned it yet
                beside the clam shacks

        where the men all act
alluring and young.

Now, As Ever

The sun has done
its job for today,
resuscitating ruins,

staring back at the bright
eye of the pool,
blue goal, flipped sky.

Two holes of water, everyone outside.
We wanted the dead for ourselves
and here they are.

From far away,
where everything stays,
the peals of industry

swell as daylight fades.
When evening greets
the costumed guests,

everyone asked is a blessing.
Tonight, says one, *comes closer than before*,
his hand circling his mask,

what took so long. Cunning and flirting
with relevance, the moon intones,
Why bother, bothered, with description—

it has always been this way.
Oh, bent moon, how you
do go on.

Duplicate lanterns quiver
in the long-winded wind—night's
another entrance, don't swallow.

Birds of Prayer

The tiniest inkling of tenderness
exhumed by a blink:
    What bird is it lives below ground
    and which of us finds his best use?

    When red calculations, hidden and hinged,
lift, a bargaining
    throat proclaims from the stable trees.
    But is this not the way error

    arranges itself? The contessa needs
a new pair of doves.
    And then there were two scarecrow types—
    one you loved and the other you

    held inside your mouth like a wish. Look at
the effort preserved
    in this bright spectacle of leaves,
    a map of claws you can follow.

    According to the trees, all's credible,
lightwise, between them.
    The ground moves below us—we glance
    at what holds us up and lose track.

    It's been raining, but not so we could hear.
Wings bearing pure verbs
    skirt the drops that fall on windmills
    asleep in their own exact hands.

Jersey

The optimism of a parking lot,
the miles all heaped up and stuck together
like so much rice. O Tiffany Wigs, O
Psychic Readings, beware one-stop shopping.

In a bus on the turnpike, I open
my mouth—my reflection in the window
swallows the headlights of oncoming cars.
What, never eaten a pomegranate?

They're not worth the fuss. No one admits this.
But I have grown inured to the droning
engines, tires spinning me almost asleep,
various mouthbreathers dazed at the wheel.

A billboard boasts Televised Autopsies,
the odor of wet leaves circles my head.
The lit verbiage fuses, leading to
serendipitous misunderstandings

in a row of pietàs. Do we want
rapture or to snorkel in backyard pools?
Here is how we beg: silent, faces masked
in sheer panty hose.   Some would call us thieves.

Leaving for Good/Enjoying the Ride

One of the conjoined twins mutters,
Stop that blasted singing, to which
the other replies, *Compromise*—

you will say tiger
lily and mean body
of something on the roadside,

that part of it, the eye. Then she downshifts
into a torchy ballad. The candles glow
in plastic milk jugs

arrayed on the lawn and the first boy
removes his shirt at a party inside.
Back out on the main road,

where Dykes Lumber cozies up
to Skinner's Nuts, everything is feasible
and I'm skittish as a fruit fly on a soda gun.

But for now, your skin, my reserve—how
'bout a little Mexican moonlight,
a tray of petits fours, anything but this.

Mesh

If ever an enterprise
were doomed —
What was told to me:
gingerbread (poisoned),

strangers crushing
bric-a-brac,
I needn't have died
as many times.

Also heard of hazard
and love, the sky
over there fills with them.
One to here knows

when, another to rue
the whirl. I endure,
merely, a forger
in the red beam.

As One Might Have Kissed a Girl
One Meant Goodbye

Illusionist this adheres
to nothing no excuse
for such enclosure
thrown over and over (this going)

Who will make the unstuck relic stick

Trip into the waving
blow and disappear
full of commands
all for us

Not many appellations left so
into the sinkhole in chains we go
maybe down there
there's one that fits

O christ unmentionable
here bring the rowboat the grainy footage
the real audience

Zoom in close and see what frays
what rusts

Ether a familiar gesture

Water the heartbeat the licking legs

2

Life is inevitably disgusting.

—W.H. Auden

Groupie

All the money I lied about, the makeshift
stomach pump—forget everything

and the way to where it happened. The guitar
god wants me/has me/ditches me/calls me

from the road and can I wire some money, he's
gotten into a situation: a barren tour-bus fridge

so can I meet him in Trenton and bring a bag.
The next nude reveals herself

and she's thin in the way the age demands—
not conventionally pretty, not conventionally shaved,

but a rail to rail against if there's time and there is.
I'm at work on a new line of lipsticks—Foie Gras,

Primordial Soup, Contusion—everyone who tries them
gets beautiful.

The girls and I wanted to be famous,
instead we love an astronaut who blows

sunshine up our asses from halfway to its source. Fuck him.
Our supply lines have snapped—no more K, no more X,

no more. I take comfort in gossip, the usual
gossip, but different: this one stitched a quilt of moths,

another painted all his rooms gold. We, the girls and I,
we pull the wings off swan boats, follow our favorite

to the stars and the capsule in which we keep
recipes we've saved for our successors so they do not starve.

No Nets

Distorted self in thunder
and the sound stalks off—
so, too, iffily, the cumuli.
The notorious run all over
this island in their paper
dresses painted purple and Stanley Kubrick,
it snowed on the desert
the day he was born.
—Whilst ferrying the brass band
—During a long stroll in the garden
—After the silk screens were forced
His murder was a mystery full of twists
written on a dressing-room wall.
~~No more handjobs "on the house."~~
One has only reverb now.

Continuity

Why, then, the sun where it should hang at noon
as a TV mother carves a roast for dinner?

And why the crack of thunder hours
before the lightning hits?

Furthermore the whole sky
mad with smoke and ash

from a single tree struck.
Why does he read over my shoulder when

he's got his copy open to the same page?
As one inhales it's him

and not the mother
and it's turkey and it's frozen.

Breathe out, he leads a song in the terraced
garden, all the girls on cue—but the one

in back is now in front and weren't
they all arranged by height?—singing, *Mother*

is it turtle soup again? They scatter when
they hear the caterpillars'

grinding in the trees.

For This I Went to College

I am holding the telephone to my head,
the very model of semiprofessional
courtesy. First the voice

made entirely of electricity, next
a collect call from Nigeria pulling me in.
Are you The Yes Man?

I would like to be The Yes Man too.
I'm what? Important? Flatterer
(from the Old French: *to lick*).

My ear all day
a tide pool
where stars gather.

We have a new arrangement today—
lilies that, come Thursday,
will peel back to simulate gagging.

Dusty little tongues.
Consider antimatter
as a verb,

phrenology as a day of the week.
Shit rolls downhill.
I'm here to catch it.

Breakdown

Dragging a blunt in his bedroom, a dashing bumboy dreams of David Bowie, deadbolts the decibels. He drinks booze like Bette Davis (Benedictine, Drambuie) and Blanche DuBois (bourbon). Baudelaire beats a drum and a bodybuilder blows a double bassoon while brain-dead dreamboats brandish bulky daisies and bounce on diving boards in the boondocks—a delicate balancing. Dearly beloved, don't let the bedbugs bite your daily bread. Don't be a douchebag or deny a dog a bone. Disbelief becomes delirium when darling buds blossom in the deep blue day.

No Lot Lizards

December and the leaves fell more
out of habit than anything else.
I would let things spoil, I would wake up

in Baltimore wearing reflective pants,
an asbestos apron. *We like your style*, they said,
especially that welding mask—but tell us this:

What is the sound of Two Gals Trucking?
Another megamall is rising out of broken
earth and dirt; the engineers sprawl by the highway,

crooning one more chorus of "I'll Skip Miami"
around the Gatorade cooler. The cranes
over Chesapeake Bay await their instructions, high

in the unrepentant opalescent smog. People queue up
outside factories, wowed by specialty metals. An acid
rain wets their faces but they don't mind

because they read on the Net that it's a good
exfoliant. So goodbye pollen, goodbye spores—
here come the fetching weathermen, giving us what for.

Herethere

A tugboat tugging nothing
troubles the river on both sides,

the cleansing rain
is no such thing. Clumped and egregious,

excess reveals itself in the vale—
a tease of unending,

the desert another expression of déjà vu.
We should have stayed on the bus

with our rocket, ramps
and fiddleheads and what

we knew reduced to miniature.
O monocot. O brainstem home and home.

The strolling violinist drooped
in sympathy, a ploy to hide

a different depth of air.
Home in three streets,

he's a wealth of invitations,
toes a leg during a dalliance,

I'm floored by such tender displays.
Didn't I say the jitney'd keep us pure?

We had enough of backseat intrigue—
two together, two apart,

another waits to seize what comes.
All worked on the premise

that numbers were magic,
were wrong.

Slutty

We couldn't get near the bathroom
            with all the models

holding back their hair
over the porcelain bowls.

The chef barely knew how to fling
parsley, so in the end   no one mourned

the hors d'oeuvres' demise.
The champagne was another story.

            A great mystery
to me as well you should be,

your legs seemed longer when
you cartwheeled under the streetlights:

Straddle me and I'll give you
all the gossip, all the sugar.

        —What would one do
with *all* the sugar anyway?

Caress can still be the right word,
the streets   dark and aflash

with rain   sliding through the city
on its way. A third party wants

in, that warmth. You love
the noise stars make when they fall.

In the morning   we are knocked around
by the wind   of approaching trains.

You play the drawn-on eyebrow,
    you play the figure-me-out—

I'd like something too
    to tear at me.

Projections

The night topples, I believe it started
in the noodle shop and ended
without gravity and swimming
in water spiked with dye to make it more
reflective. Or perhaps another night,
a defunct city I never loved.
My secrets would expose me
as the tedious creature I had once
meant to grow into.
      Overheard this time,
the girl with the sun in her head
glides by but sunless, clear,
suggesting an unstable nature
—that it might always be so—
energy, energy, used indiscriminately.
Clean up, tighten; break some, be broken.
The portrait-makers perpetuate
the oddest spectator sport—
isn't it morning here already?
No wonder the subjects
are sullen and twitch
under all this counterfeit light.

The Whore of Binghamton

Put my dollar in the jukebox cat
sniffing my pumps keen for the fish
bones I spiked in an alley behind Hunan Palace

with a guy who said I was an exotic bird
and it's partly true I like shiny things
so I stole his watch as I blew him.

You get three songs here all of mine
are going to be long. Here's one about
a handbag in a tire track and a gone moon

that puts me back at 15 my legs antennae
stabbing a half-moon through the sunroof
of some shitty Trans Am under

the oak in my mother's driveway.
She took the money blacked my eye
said *Hell's half fulla whores like you*

so I made a snow angel by the front porch
watched it stand up and thrash her dead
with its wings and I was gone.

Should I have been born a boy slingshooting rats
and fingering girls like me down by the oil tanks
well maybe I was. I know all the secret spots.

I'll bad sister you by the airstrip and pull
out the bullet with my teeth your finger
in the slit of my skirt will mean it then and so will I.

A Little Education Goes a Long Way

R. is lately taken
with the abyss, invoking
Kierkegaard's notion of
the despair of possible infinity
v. the despair of infinite possibility.
We agree that any artist
worth/with a grain of salt
must face the latter
and set to fashioning variations
of our own (the infinite
possibility of despair).
I begin an essay on this
as it is manifested in popular music
("So Many Men, So Little Time").
But since I've been obsessed
with ice cream lately, I abandon
it in favor of one on which poets
liked ice cream (Schuyler)
and which ones did not (O'Hara).
To do this properly, I stop
reading their poems
and provide no footnotes.
Dead poets only—
that way, they can't
call me up and say,
Hey jerk blah blah blah blah blah.
Of course, they'd only be talking
to my answering machine, next to
which I may or may not be
asleep, a magazine
covering my face.

Ethics

The three-year-old girl clings
to the back of a car. *Do it*

again do it again, the reporters
chant. It's a hot day for April,

a membrane coats the lens.

What part of _____
does she not understand?

How about learning disabled—
can we say that?

And can we get someone to re-
enact the bit with the hot spoons

on the retarded sister's legs?

In one commercial the legatees
were dapper and kissed

like madmen. Let us not
blame them for our sorrows—

for aren't they like any of us
just waiting to learn which

of the oceans would be most
receptive to their advances?

It would appear the psychic-
hotline gals have all gone

on strike—anything to
excuse this recent fortune.

Hiatus

You have given up on your hands.
Gone are the days of cupping,
gone are the nights of wringing.
The era of holding has passed.
What you take with you:
what fits in your mouth.
                    O the treats.
Going down,
the stairwell smells of toothpaste—
someone is planning ahead.
                    You weren't
trying to build something
lovely but the words were there
                    and not there.
What else could we do
but scare you away?
          Fillings falter.
          Radios rebel.
What you have left us:
the voices of taxi dispatchers
          bouncing off the night.

3

Blasted Fields of Clover Bring
Harrowing and Regretful Sighs

Now the sea moves up the lawn for him as those nearby view his life passing before their eyes. Someone his own age lean in black pants and a white shirt sits on a plastic chair with a block of massive green light. Facing of someone else away (bluebird). This is not happening to him. Unaccountable ejaculation. Briefs halted at the knees alter his walk. The basement conceals a surplus of chairs while overground the yards remain square and trimmed to uniform length (clouds). This was written on his arm. Its words occupy a grid and move among cells at random with great speed. A car leaves a driveway and exclamations are made about wood left over and what could make it burn.

Stacked circles (rain down) say green it releases nothing. Bundled wires. Ellsworth Kelly strides from one red iceberg to the next. Each face projects onto antennae forging a domain expressed as a skewered pod. Transparency behind a desk elusive plunge. A dissection of thought into its components the weight of meat up the wrong street the wrong back door. The blazer missed too as the wiry one observed. Someone slipped him diet Orangina and he went ballistic. The whole staff crayoned their names onto the good-luck card while unwitting party-goers waited for the elevator. Mogul and musician separated at birth one suggested. Hubris. The directions were specific and yet so many stood idle. She ravished in black. He charmed in lime.

Favored lambs in a personal ad bend forward onto their knees as a peon carries the wrong box away. His employer emerges from a hole with his tan seersucker muddied holding galleys and leading a greener trainee. The spectator's disruption drew a reprimand. Distance to the beach in relation to time of departure conveyed in a series of double-jointed hand signals wasted on recruits. One shoved another flirtatiously. Water just off the porch did not suffice. Suspended above it the chef's diorama betrayed him with silk flowers. The man who played wolf in the film version lived next door and perfect sand lay just over the crest where no one made excuses for skin upon skin or lip balm crushed into a cap. Again the lambs' complaints drift on a pink foam from the hollow. A magazine a wrong night a chance meeting what is owed biting at elbows and ropes.

As a shopping cart careened the football team scattered. Next year they'll find changes of clothes in the woods. When the dandy rode his horse-drawn carriage through the W. Village (1969) he was roundly egged. The feathers of his headdress destroyed. His little dogchild keening mommy&daddy over and over would mind no one but him. He denied raiding Sarduy as he nursed the whiny cur. Each headshot a different era the nipple still surprised. Those along the canal tried to keep windows clean. Friends on the phone in the same room hardly knew. Another back turned to a picture window. One man in Confederate garb fingered Julia's necklace and grazed her breast. Thus was his gall not unlike that of an older queen who'd sprung out of a hedge nude from the waist down. Who was pushed in first. Teeter on a narrow strip of grass. Here little dogchild here.

Rain focuses primarily on the hive. Adirondack chairs within persist in their vacancy. Their metal tubes. Labyrinthine restroom beside the only traffic light in town. A discrete unit. Shopping opportunities within the hive but most walk counterclockwise around the perimeter. Groups gather to spin matching umbrellas and this precedes their movement back to transports then home or what signifies home. Most endangered are the small cakes. Wander with averted intention. Confusion at the counter. Everyone given something to hoist or conceal. Sprinklers activate themselves washing away crumbs. Up on a hill at the edge of the woods a shadow raised its sword. One vocalist hides behind a partition to pull out a heart and sing it to sleep.

When the highway turns into a shrimp-processing plant remove the scooters from the roof of the car. Downward slope facilitates a guided tour. How antennae and entrails cling to the stainless steel floors in tiny pools. Glasses match a curl of hair. Recipe in the backseat. Every auditorium is a high-school auditorium. Algae in the canals and a lack of wind hindered the ships and spoiled the race but ropes remain suited to their use. Long night for the union. Some revel in leaving behind no more than a history of woe. Joined like crabs the sensation travels through clothing and causes a shudder then infamy. Long night. One of them backed over the dragon with his car. Even as he brushed his hair over the page.

The aspiring lothario braves red jellies in the surf. Touch and break. Stipple and fix. The Russian woman has seen the prince on television so she slaps him. The glass dome gives way revealing suspicion of holidays. On the table gifts pack and unpack. An instrument crushed on the floor next to a video screen with its loop of sparks. Forensics identify it as cello or harp removed by its perpetrators the two guilty brothers. Potpourri in a mylar bag clicks with bees though the merchant vows innocence even as one crawls into the mouth of the giver. When a c-list actor arrives at a restaurant everyone lies to him about his cream sweater. Stairs lead to minor judgments and more rain visible at night. Someone has done the worst thing.

They gave the old bastard a Pulitzer but stopped short of naming him king. Children play board meeting and use pretzel rods for cigars facilitating the decision-making process. Coffee is a fruity ruby punch. The nerve center of the Spearmint Rhino in the warehouse district. An institution where gentlemen give five dollars to bored syphilitic whores wrapped around metal poles and every drink weighs eight pounds. More oil must be divined in order to build windmills. Desert billboards epitomize cause and effect. Totally Nude/Pregnant and Scared? By hawk or by crow. A mother leaves her blue-tongued boy on the bobsled ride and cannot find her car. Amidst the dust and animal cries he walks the length of huge transparent wings.

From the crater rose a dinosaur with girly hands. All fled to the teller machine having seen the meteor's descent a metal streak across the sky. Even the radio shrink made haste following his forehead. Rows of women in a field extol the virtues of mail-order grains. One mounts a screed another makes a wild rice portrait of her beloved sitcom neighbor. After accident and indecision they wait in a roadside shack with television and folding chairs. The breakfast contingent dwindles so the delinquent must find a new haunt. Not this time. A pizza grows colder upon each traversal of woods a mnemonic for sex and further sex on basement steps. The doll's death certificate conceals a robotic arm and by the time someone finds a phone the corn will be up to the raptor's ribs. Lackluster composure another left behind.

Vanilla milkshakes carve a canyon. Difficulty of trains flying ahead on wires dislocating breakfronts and flattening coins even the strongest can't contend. Voices of saints and restaurateurs drift down from the supermarket speakers so these must be lullabies. Mind the fruit with terrible hackles. Never the kiwi too. No one can hold the tweezers steady in this wind. Silver. The cabbie with cauliflower ear and nose makes a drastic U-turn and berates his passengers in the rearview mirror. See as they run uphill their legs can barely move. The devil's hands make idols and into coffee grinders he throws them. His face culled for a German lantern later auctioned off. One of his minions disgorges five black beetles onto a maple kitchen floor.

Emerald carpet on the balcony. A false diva's hair frizzed on the plane and befreckled flight attendants pulled out their eyedrops over the Rockies. In front of the firehouse a burly officer ranted barking and advancing toward a family gathered on the restaurant stairs. He comported himself with rage. You cunt one of the boys piped up. They crumbled laughing but the lawman burst. Only the suitor who could retrieve the gnocchi from the pool in one motion would win the daughter's hand. It wasn't Ray a grade-A flibbertigibbet with numerous keys and enormous tonsils. His exit interview dragged on for hours. Security leaned into their tabloids and that night he came in a sailor's hair short sailor hair.

In its wateriness the confection persisted. In its vat it swirled. Kevin decided to take the next flight ordered a sausage and ran to watch the planes descend and rise. Godspeed You Black Emperor skewed a flower shop's ambiance and the proprietress inexpertly patched a cardboard record sleeve. Slow now heavy throat wrong end of a microphone pressed in the hollow. Traditions cast themselves aside in hopes of being collected and hung in galleries. Perplexed the grandmother-to-be expanded. Church and more church the only remedy. Paths appeared between lengthening streets. Symbolism sufficed. A second matron fretted above ham steaks as the long-lost embraced the girls then resumed his place at the grill. Waiters orbit the periphery baffled by fate. What is my section what is my role one asked of the ample dyke. Doomed flight of the bombers then. Vodka froze. Just a wave.

From hotel bar to hotel bar no one could describe the Fifth Amendment with sufficient confidence. Elders upped their cultural sensitivity in vain. Mary and her guitar on the swinging ladder could get no answers about kin flying in from Dover. Perhaps the vast parking lot held clues. The cuckold knew sharks lurked in the rapids and even retrieved a boy's rudder when it snapped off. He invented names for all the fish in the arroyo. Those who escaped the skits found the hotel sat on a cliff with no warnings. Earth just ends. Who will claim discarded teeth and who has sufficient nerve to extract the shard from his own palm. All day the sour clerk willfully ignored requests then snuck off to verify Stevie at the other end of his voice. No one but no one can drive up such an incline without falling off.

(Mary Hansen 1966-2002)

Nothing blurred as he stepped over the stones. The raft pinched his legs numb in false rapids. Water striders opened the surface tolerance for cold for needles for knives. Get thee to a cannery homunculus lovebird while those who recall the speaker of an old Kinnell chestnut eating bearshit have a good laugh at the reunion over Harvey Wallbangers. Drunk as a president's daughter. Consumption like fun she got the clap come a growl from a middle row. The driver rotated making the children nervous and she lost her bus in a comical skid. The rest of the circle begged off as a curse was yelled into a deli but no two witnesses concurred. Chime chime chime. Night rides day as though the crown of the earth had slipped.

When the curmudgeon says so-and-so is greazy Billy who's been dead for years finds it hilarious. Greazy. Whaddya have honey. A sign once perched over a bed now hangs properly over a highway hawking pills. All the lotions stacked in footnotes. An ocelot patrols the ditch for golden carp that swim upstream and lunges at the scent of human on the other side of a plexiglass wall. Under the hero's parachute the spaceship shrunk revealing there could not have been much or many inside. A hole opened and he wore the vehicle like a hat. Rain along the road and parked lost cars. Only women were secure as drops collected. Paranoid royals clothed erotic secrets in brambles then spread them out over a field.

An Austrian porn star afterward gathered ruined polaroids of the northern ends of volcanic islands. The bride on the tour boat perched atop a yellow plastic slide ready for her new life. Photos were found lodged in a menu and tarps were hauled in. Organs migrated. Smile across a dirty corridor piss crept from under the booths. A spider took up residence in the sink preparing for her thousand babies. Branches held egg sacs clusters of poison berries. Old acquaintances compared their shaved chests and coyly slipped beneath covers. The widow's hands shook as she searched her inventory of jokes spilling coffee on the detective her husband's only surviving amigo. The bride she drowned.

Over a mound of black popcorn two girls tossed their red hair then piled back into the bus to follow a joke metal band farther into the woods. Men exposed there by flashlight beams. Animals clung to bark and shifted shapes. As he swung from the bars on the subway car an obese boy endeavored to kick his fellow passengers while his guardian skulked and glared. Tip of thorn stuck in his finger lent an evangelical air. Burmese prisoners wearing wooden armor that linked them together like an old escalator were made to row an enormous boat. Some escapees piled into a station wagon that teetered off a cliff into the sea but they rolled down their windows and swam to shore. How blue the space above. Ex-lovers picked fights on platforms over whether a lemon's truth is the zest or the flesh. How wide.

4

Beauty makes me hopeless.

—Anne Carson

And You Thought You Were the Only One

Someone waits at my door. Because he is
      dead he has time but I have my secrets—

      this is what separates us from the dead.
See, I could order take-out or climb down

the fire escape, so it's not as though he
      is keeping me from anything I need.

      While this may sound like something I made up,
it is not; I have forgotten how to

lie, despite all my capable teachers.
      Lies are, in this way, I think, like music

      and all is the same without them as with.
The fluid sky retains regret, then bursts.

He is still there, standing in the hall, insisting
      he is someone I once knew and wanted,

      come laden with gifts he cannot return.
If I open the door he'll flash and fade

like heat lightning behind a bank of clouds
      one summer night at the edge of the world.

Pounce

He's the prettiest thing I've ever seen/
synthetic boy/imploding star.
You can't swing a dead fish

and expect to split the dissonance.
An ego unhinged by chemicals/
the prettiest thing I've ever seen.

The seconds commiserate and pounce/
oh I am but a simple tramp I know/
in underground rivers forgotten fish

glow. I've seen a future there
in the skittish projections/his eyes
the prettiest eyes I've ever seen.

He slid down a mountain of steel
to drop his bread in the sea
and I went to where the fish

return before they replicate and die.
I would ask no more of the world/
the prettiest thing I've ever seen
flattens my heart like scales on fish.

Not Again

<blockquote>

The interview was about to begin,
I went for a walk instead.

</blockquote>

Someone does not say, *Sorry I missed you*
because he isn't, doesn't,

<blockquote>

and as usual everyone's relish-
ing specifics except me.

</blockquote>

The sun seems plausible for the first time —
I don't even miss the park

<blockquote>

when it folds itself up like a blanket
with all its secrets intact,

</blockquote>

coinciding with a quest for better
and even better yet things —

<blockquote>

they put an office here for a reason
though this too is easily

</blockquote>

negated. The trees, with all they have seen,
are getting ready to call

<blockquote>

it a day, which it is. They'll sing toward night,
where someone might be waiting.

</blockquote>

Neither *Just* nor *Like*

If all cities are made of light, then what?
Champagne on the sidewalk,
we drink to the eclipse
and kick the black edge
of a loading dock
with the backs of our feet.
Watch his legs.

———

A kiss comes up
in the lesbian bar.
Then some bad news,
which in this story
I ignore.

———

A skater drums
on a cardboard box.
I can see his smile
from here. The street
soft underfoot,
a place where light is kept.

———

He's exposed
as another perennial
bad-boy type.
What a look from him holds,
holds off.

———

And I say, *Maybe*,
hanging off the edge of his bed.
He will gather

or not.
Seems to like the laces on my shoes.

———

He: undressing.

———

Me (no longer
subject but being
being acted upon):
should stop this.

———

It feels safer on the couch,
isn't. The light
makes several windows
on the ceiling. The fire
escape adds angles
to the shadows—his,
on his way.

———

In this weird light he wants it again.

———

A movie tilts
over the avenue.
My wanting, my wreck
and desire—may I
never regret having asked,
may I.

Immersion In and Of

Let me give you a mess of colors—they
        will not run unless
you handle them carelessly—all my frames
        are full. There is some
danger of them advancing into this
        room and that since I
am never home these days, as my message
        indicates. Saintly
but you blew it. I'm through counting on your
        dirty fingers and
I'm through watching you tram up the mountain
        to eat all the snow.
You told me something terrible happened
        and caused a sudden
shift in your aesthetic, such as it was,
        long ago. Our friend,
she of the sex-change and a fondness for
        heroin, sends love
and broken cookies from the country. It's
        a different night
where you lie down, when you lie down, no doubt.

Tuna in Spring Water

It was yet another of your schemes—
                    we'd work
three months on a commercial
fishing boat; at the end
we'd have enough dough
                    to move on
          to the next adventure.
                              Sheer hell,
sounded like to me.
You were all talk, anyway,
and by the end,
                    not even that.
As for the labels on these cans,
they perplex me.
                    I try to make something
          of the letters.
Where did I get this fear
of doing things?
                    Pretty soon,
someone notices
the missing pills,
how late it is.
          And like that.
Then you're (meaning "one's")
                              pulled in,
as by the eddies
                    around a ship
barely visible
on a horizon.
                    No one would know.
                    No accounting for thirst.
I drain the water from a can
of tuna into the cat's dish
                    and he licks it up
                    with little licking sounds.

The Ice along the Road

And nothing we could ever lose
spreads over the white ground.
Soft ellipses of footprints lead
into the trees—

more will follow. You imagined
tears—not mine—either way,
a dearth of postcards you would not
want to reveal.

This night forgot us years ago,
but could not wait you out.
Violet candies crumble on
the window ledge;

the birds return for them, deceived.
I need you to tell me
the orange smoke of the plastics
factory is

beautiful against the moon and
that all you want is to
sleep the rest of the way with your
head on my lap.

After the Smoke Cleared

we emerged nostalgic for the various fruits
of youth,
for nostalgia.

When X died we held sway
as a pack of dogs
carried on beyond the trees—

no reprimand,
only the tacit threat of tooth and foam.
The drunker we got

the drunker we got.
Someone woke him up that night,
he told me, a hand

across his mouth,
as if, were he to cry out,
they would find him.

Goddamn dogs, man.
You don't know.
We take fear less seriously now,

having passed into a lull of cautious optimism.
We make love in hot tubs
and look down

at the lights below,
peach and diffuse under smog.
Since the gods went missing

we have had to amuse ourselves, alas.
At least no one gets older anymore.
Having never found our way,

we can nonetheless retreat
into the sound of wind badgering leaves,
always portending more of the same.

Fledglings

A boy finds a white bird
in a white box and calls
it a museum.

——

The bird makes
sounds more speech than song
but not yet words so the boy
fills them in:
*Water calms the one hand desire
bends the other.*

——

The boy walks through the city,
bird on his shoulder.
Messages worded like telegrams
appear on the side of a building,
making everyone anxious.

——

The bird is stolen and replaced
by an exact replica.

——

Once the bird brings a note in its beak:

Dear Inertia,

*Thank you
for your letter please
do not write to me again.*

> *Faithfully,*
> *Ton Petit Oiseau*

——

The bird learns to operate
a series of levers
embedded in the boy's skull.

————

The boy is apparently in love

(—certain phrases have grown indistinct
since you carved them on me here take
                    your shank
            upside down
    I am equally tractable—)

even if this does not sound like love.

————

They both

————

fly south.

————

The inside of the boy's refrigerator
is lined with photographs of the bird.

————

In a restaurant they share
a slice of berry pie.
The boy enjoys the filling,
the bird prefers the crust.

————

At first the boy wondered
if the bird was
a reincarnation
but he understands
better now the properties
of the fabric of the soul.

————

It has been noted
that the bird more closely resembles
a cockatoo than a dove.

———

The boy's skin emits light
as a quarry wall in darkness does
when struck by the moon.

———

The boy has sold some of the bird's
feathers to disreputable characters
who claim that, given the right
conditions of light, they have witnessed
a phenomenon in which an image
of the box, long ago discarded,
appears around the bird.
From what angle and how long,
one might ask with the same mouth.

———

The boy now carries a painting
of the bird on someone else's shoulder.
When it rains—and it is always raining—
droplets form as they would
on real feathers and roll off.

Truncated Elegy

Before going under   did he notice   how the sky grew

thick with the wings of birds   or taste the rust of lungs   the ache

We wait by the delta for a drunken boy to return

leaving our doors unlocked in case his longing exceeds us

To have shifted abandon   into something tangible —

a manna to prevail against cognition's undertow

Flower in his teeth   love sung to his own end   and the dark

he drifted through   like the moon burning   up a merlot sky

Jeff Buckley (1966–1997)

5

*and there's never been an opportunity to think of it as an idyll
as if everyone'd been singing around me*

—Frank O'Hara

Knowing You Could Is Better Than
Knowing You Will

I must see you; let's meet at the fringes of respectability
at quarter past nine. We could straddle the oft-licked
curb (it's the repetition we like). I promise not to say
anything louche when you buss the backs of my fingers.

What is that noise coming from the other side of the river—
maybe pavement being set perfectly straight or a woozy guitar.
In light like this we become automatic and can reach each other—
what a difficult noise to hold and clearly making love is all that.

Juiced, I'm sure we're taller than before and don't miss
what we've lost. Meanwhile the streetlights blush
in their globes as if they could tell how the party towed us
along like a chain of rollerblading kids latched onto a bus.

Later let's go swimming down by the electrical plant
since as you know the water runs out warmest from its pipes.
Bring on the horse tranquilizers
for my listing heart is pecker-fretted, truculent and true.

A Mouth of Sundays

Heaven falls like paint from a sagging ceiling.
If you miss me, pussycat, if you need me,
I'll be waiting down by the broken mailbox,
           sniffing for letters.

Leave me nothing. This is what makes me happy.
Love has seen us crow in an awkward hour as
through the walls a radio softly burbled
           "Killing Me Softly."

From the airport you are describing glints of
winter lightning, weather to fall in bed by.
When you leap the width of our sloppy country
           I do not follow.

Wing-beats try me under the open window,
Paris beckons, everyone's leaving shortly.
I will guide them, waving my rusty flashlight
           over the ocean.

Not Looking: Incunabular

flaw in weather   holds me under
then won't   I won't clutch
so harried   these elements
smear   no notwithstanding

initial stroke   passage into
who became   shroud underwater
am one of   rescinded
burnish or elide   veracity
bared hands   burst and liquid
                    fish contort
and die of air   anatomy
on the surface   series of breaths
good for drowning   and through it
mirrorlike   oil prisms
I could anoint   myself with
still no

           but in his center
one might   ever prevail

twist my neck   to see
his neck   streaked with meteors

By the Skin of Our Luck

I used to ride around in the hole
in your lapel. From there I could watch

the fires climb out of the dumpsters
and into the sky while you caught

cinders on your tongue like snow.
I felt safe when I figured out

what you actually wanted,
despite the odd aerosol can

exploding in the night behind us
and the pleasure of your hand

sometimes finding me though otherwise
you let me pretend I was hidden.

The sun followed us all the way
to Mallorca, as did the lone helicopter

that trails me to this day.
I don't even hear it anymore

but I see what it does to the surface
of the water and your hair

and I'm sorry—you thought it was
your fault, didn't you, all those years.

A Way to Build It

Orion's belt loops around the tip of a sky-
    scraper and starts to slip down its
        length, a cincture of light:

but there are other ways to define a body:
    for example, rivers unwave
        under our scrutiny

and could be made of something other than water:
    the sirens we followed here have
        begun to sing to us

like struck tuning forks and the searchlights bend around
    our bodies as the sounds pass through,
        charging our ribcages:

the solace of mint and ginger will see us home
    in cars that mold our shapes to those
        of the night we move through:

now it is ending with our making believe sleep:
    the genius of your blowing on
        my heart to slow it down

Not Looking: Gold Course

arcs of milk   blue in layers

        extra sense

through which to take

      make teleutons of   their six names

atomize   not know   when to stop

    dust and clouded

          nebulae condense

      caught stars

shake this room

         another galaxy

   by extension

a rattle full   of dots of gold

swarming   resonance

apposite portals   but seamless

         we lean

    toward love

Anodyne Slide

I was reading about a drug that induces
immortality and causes a terrible rash—

as Giacometti said of suicide by fire,
That would be something.

Someone enumerates the ways to improve
his medicine then folds

me in half and spirits me off. Our
reputation exceeds us—word comes down

from hills somewhere near the Black Forest.
He wears a lead-paint warning sign

around his neck—an in-joke I want
out of. Nevertheless I run with him across

the Autobahn when he says, *Go.*
At the bar he orders shark

extract served in glass ampoules.
He assures me no sharks were

harmed to obtain it, but seduced
and milked over a period

of a hundred years. After a series
of trains we step into a new

city. I tell him he's gone
translucent, he laughs and runs away.

He comes back with fistfuls of pills
and says, *Come on, we're going*

to Cuba where like everywhere else
mansions fall deeper into disrepair

even as I am telling you about it now.
I'll show you: birds

and urchins cling to the rafters,
no one would look for us there.

Yes vines dangle from the trees.
Yes the tiles are coming loose.

Open wide your throat, he says,
the turning world.

7-Minute Song

Before he left but after he let
me undo the snaps he looked
at me through a porthole said
I forgive you put this light in
your mouth and maybe I'd have
taken that from Lou Reed at 21
down by the piers the Hudson
red as the boat against which
he'd pin me and pull
the river over my head.

The Extended Lights

Let's return where killer whales lingered
in three feet of water and we could not move.

Let's tread up the hill
past men who wait among the trees—

in darkness we will learn
what we wanted from them.

Let's open
our mouths to the blue rain

then break into a trampoline park
under the extended light of the Cape.

Let's reel before sounds
that fill the ballroom and beams

that strike star-balloons
revolving on their cords.

Let's drink gin rickeys
in a hotel bar below street level

then pry up frozen puddles
for the windows of our museum.

We'll record messages in the fountain
around which the rest of the garden turns

while a bird no longer than a key watches us
from his perch upon a clamshell rendered in jade.

Let's bring an empire to its knees.
Let's go back to 11:32

on a night last June when your arm fell across
my shoulder and you asked how long you could stay.

This is where I have been waiting,
waiting here for you.

Not Looking: Helical

across intellect
    or what's left of it
        cows
            forsaken
                on the hill
            affect or impediment
        in any case
    not allegory
power lines
    invariable hum
        no more
            twist in subplot
                nests unravel
            come back
        every billboard
      sky collapsing
thousand miles
    radio hurdle
        spin by
            cannot tell you
                wind unwinding
            bombast exhausted
        the other dark
      the other long
set alight briefly
    had I anything
        to give
            anything
              yours

Overheard

Boards of Canada
The Breeders
The Creatures
Brian Eno
Goldfrapp
Low
My Bloody Valentine
Orbital
Stereolab
Underworld

Acknowledgments

American Letters and Commentary, Barrow Street, Boston Review, Columbia, Fort Necessity, Good Foot, Hotel Amerika, The James White Review, Maisonneuve, NCZ, The Nebraska Review, The Paris Review, Pierogi Press, Pleiades, Poetry, Post Road, Salonika, Spork, Verse, Western Humanities Review, The Yale Review

Can We Have Our Ball Back? (canwehaveourballback.com)
The Cortland Review (cortlandreview.com)
Logopoeia (logopoeialogopoeia.da.ru)
Nerve (nerve.com)
Slope (slope.org)

Some of these poems appeared in *6 Amerikanere af Lave* (Arena, Denmark, 2001), in conjunction with the "In the Making" conference. Danish translation by Lars Bukdahl.

An excerpt from "Blasted Fields of Clover Bring Harrowing and Regretful Sighs" was published in *Great American Prose Poems: From Poe to the Present* (Scribner, 2003). David Lehman, ed.

"Knowing You Could Is Better Than Knowing You Will," "Slutty" and "Tingling in the Extremities" were published in *Word of Mouth: An Anthology of Gay American Poetry* (Talisman House, 2000). Timothy Liu, ed.

MARK BIBBINS teaches writing workshops at The New School, where he also co-founded *LIT* magazine. His work has appeared in many anthologies and magazines, including *Poetry*, the *Paris Review*, the *Yale Review*, and *Take Three: 3*. He lives in New York City.

This book was designed by Rachel Holscher. It is set in Electra type by Stanton Publication Services, Inc., and manufactured by Bang Printing on acid-free paper.